The Hidden Names Of Genesis Tap Into The Hidden Power Of Manifestation

Copyright information

Copyright © 2015 by Baal Kadmon

All rights reserved. No part of this book may be reproduced by any mechanical, photographic, or electrical process, or in the form of a recording. Nor may it be stored in a storage/retrieval system nor transmitted or otherwise be copied for private or public use-other than "fair use" as quotations in articles or reviews—without the prior written consent of the Author.

The Information in this book is solely for educational purposes and not for the treatment, diagnosis or prescription of any diseases. This text is not meant to provide financial or health advice of any sort. The Author and the publisher are in no way liable for any use or misuse of the material. No Guarantee of results are being made in this text.

Kadmon, Baal

The Hidden Names Of Genesis- Tap Into The Hidden Power Of Manifestation

−1st ed

Printed in the United States of America

Cover image : © nikola-master - Fotolia.com
Book Cover Design: Baal Kadmon

At the best of our ability we have credited those who created the pictures based on the research we have conducted. If there are images in the book that have not been given due copyright notice please contact us at Resheph@baalkadmon.com and we will remedy the situation by giving proper copyright credit or we will remove the image/s at your request.

INTRODUCTION

What you are about to learn is known by VERY few people. In fact, you will not find anything about this online. Some might even say that what you will read in this book is not true. That is for you to decide. I gather that if you apply what you learn, you will realize the truth of these words. If you feel it has not helped you, you can always return this book. I assure you, however, that you will be one of the very few who know this power and I suspect it will work for you as well. It seems to work for everyone who learns it.

If you have read my other books "The 72 Names Of God", "The 72 Angels Of The Name" and "The 99 Names Of Allah" you will know that the power of divine names contain the essence of all existence. When you have the name of the divine, you possess a key to divine power.

In this book, you will learn, for the first time, the 6 hidden names of God within the first few verses in the book of Genesis. The names are in Hebrew, but do not worry. I will transliterate as necessary. These names are known by VERY few people. Today, you will learn them for yourself.

Although the old testament books are filled with secret names of the divine, the ones in the book of Genesis are of utmost importance. Why? The book of Genesis is the account of divine creation. God manifested the entire universe and it is recounted allegorically and some would say literally, within the pages of Genesis. This significant because the hidden names are the very names God used for creation. By tapping into these names, you will have a piece of the power used in the Genesis of the universe. You can use the power of Genesis, to manifest whatever it is you require in your life. It is, after all, the book of creation...Isn't it?

CHAPTER 1: THE NAME IS THE KEY

When someone calls your name, do you turn around? Does the person calling your name have your attention? Do you realize that when someone calls your name and you respond, that is them exerting a kind of power over you? You are giving them attention by the mere fact of them calling your name. When they call your name, you respond. Although you have the option not to respond, the hearing of your name will cause a reaction within you. Your ears perk up...Don't they? Its automatic, autonomic...instinctive... Try it, call someone's name. How will they respond? Will they respond with..."Yes?" Or "What?". Do you see the power in this?

This phenomena holds true with the divine. When you call upon the divine name/s you are going to bring about a response. Unlike our names, however, divine names have an extra element. They represent a spiritual power very much like electricity. Its neither good nor bad, but when its called forth, it comes. It molds itself to the environment that it is called into. The same electricity powers your Television as it does your computer; yet it displays itself in different forms within both. This nature is inherent in the names of God as well. You call forth names of creation, you will induce a cascade of manifestation and creation. As they say, be careful what you ask for. In the next chapter, we will discuss the book of Genesis briefly and then the following chapter we will discuss the 6 names of God Hidden within the first critical verses with the book of Genesis itself. It's time for this secret to be revealed.

CHAPTER 2: IN THE BEGINNING WAS THE NAME

"In the beginning God created the heavens and the earth" - Genesis 1:1

The book of Genesis, the first of 5 books of the Torah or the first 5 books of the old testament is the most enigmatic book in the bible. Within its pages we learn of God's creation and the story of our earliest ancestors. So much can be said about the book of Genesis that many books can and have been written about it. Some look at this book as concrete fact and will die defending that belief and others believe it is allegorical and simply a story that is trying to capture the essence of creation. No matter what stance is taken, one must agree that its words are quite mysterious and that inside the words lurks hidden meanings, Hidden doors of perception and hidden keys to creation and manifestation. By simply looking at the Hebrew words of the first paragraph of Genesis can infuse within you the power and light of creation. In fact, the very first day of creation, a hidden light is referenced within. Most miss it, but this is the spiritual light that will infuse creation and the universe and all eternity.

In this chapter, what I am going to do is establish that the book of Genesis is , in fact, suffused with powerful secrets. I won't go through every single one of them, but will cover 2 I think are of most importance. One is an overt secret and another is covert and hidden. This will create a platform from which to establish the validity of my words for future chapters.

Now, Let us discuss...

The first secret I have just referred to. The light of creation. A light you will be tapping into shortly. Let us read the account of the first day and find this light. Its hiding in plain sight.

Genesis 1: 1-4 " 1 In the beginning God created the heavens and the earth. ² Now the earth was formless and empty, darkness was over the surface of the deep, and the Spirit of God was hovering over the waters.

³ And God said, "Let there be light," and there was light. ⁴ God saw that the light was good, and he separated the light from the darkness. ⁵ God called the light "day," and the darkness he called "night." And there was evening, and there was morning—the first day."

On the outset this sounds like a straight forward reference to the first day of creation, but no, it is not quite that straight forward. I will ask you a question, and your answer will be the key to understanding why this verse does not refer to the light as simply an aspect of day time.

What do you associate most with daytime? Perhaps Light? Yes, but what causes that light? If you live on this great earth the answer would be the Sun. So daytime is daytime because of the sun. However, if you notice, God does not make any reference to the sun. In fact, the sun wasn't even created yet. The sun is created on the fourth day...let us read.

Genesis 1: 14-19 " [14] And God said, "Let there be lights in the vault of the sky to separate the day from the night, and let them serve as signs to mark sacred times, and days and years, [15] and let them be lights in the vault of the sky to give light on the earth." And it was so. [16] God made two great lights—**the greater light to govern the day and the lesser light to govern the night**. He also made the stars. [17] God set them in the vault of the sky to give light on the earth, [18] to govern the day and the night, and to separate light from darkness. And God saw that it was good. [19] And there was evening, and there was morning—**the fourth day.**

As you see, the day and night we most refer to in our day to day lives was created on the fourth day, not the first.

The light of the first day is the divine light of creation and within that light also is contained the darkness. The yin and yang of creation as it were. Do you see? That is the hidden light of creation. Right under our noses all this time. People look and see reference to day and night but do not see that it has nothing to do with daytime or night time at all but everything to do with spiritual light of the creation. Some may even refer to this light as the moment of the big bang. Makes one ponder.

There are many secret in Genesis, but by far the most interesting one found involve something called Torah Code. Torah Codes are essentially, equally spaced letters that form meaningful passages with the biblical text. In this example, I will display a code that is not only found in Genesis, but also the other of the first 5 books of the Old testament.

The Torah, or the 5 books of Moses, in Hebrew is spelled (right to left):

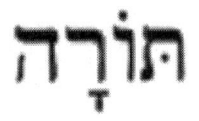

תּוֹרָה

In this example, We will find the word Torah hidden with the text of Genesis and other books of the Torah. Whoever put these books to print, hid it within the text. Divine hand perhaps?

First example: In Genesis reading right to left, if you count 50 letters from the letter in green and continue to do so for 4 letters it spells Torah. This is from Genesis 1: 1-5

א בְּרֵאשִׁית, בָּרָא אֱלֹהִים, אֵת הַשָּׁמַיִם, וְאֵת הָאָרֶץ.
ב וְהָאָרֶץ, הָיְתָה תֹהוּ וָבֹהוּ, וְחֹשֶׁךְ, עַל-פְּנֵי תְהוֹם; וְרוּחַ אֱלֹהִים, מְרַחֶפֶת עַל-פְּנֵי הַמָּיִם.
ג וַיֹּאמֶר אֱלֹהִים, יְהִי אוֹר; וַיְהִי-אוֹר.
ד וַיַּרְא אֱלֹהִים אֶת-הָאוֹר, כִּי-טוֹב; וַיַּבְדֵּל אֱלֹהִים, בֵּין הָאוֹר וּבֵין הַחֹשֶׁךְ.
ה וַיִּקְרָא אֱלֹהִים לָאוֹר יוֹם, וְלַחֹשֶׁךְ קָרָא לָיְלָה; וַיְהִי-עֶרֶב וַיְהִי-בֹקֶר, יוֹם אֶחָד. {פ}

As you see, the word Torah is spelled out every 50 letters from the last letter of the first word. Now, I understand that one could say that this is a fluke. However, it is not a fluke. Here is another example from another book of the Torah, the book of exodus.

Exodus 1: 1-6

א וְאֵלֶּה, שְׁמוֹת בְּנֵי יִשְׂרָאֵל, הַבָּאִים, מִצְרָיְמָה: אֵת יַעֲקֹב, אִישׁ וּבֵיתוֹ בָּאוּ.
ב רְאוּבֵן שִׁמְעוֹן, לֵוִי וִיהוּדָה.
ג יִשָּׂשכָר זְבוּלֻן, וּבִנְיָמִן.
ד דָּן וְנַפְתָּלִי, גָּד וְאָשֵׁר.
ה וַיְהִי, כָּל-נֶפֶשׁ יֹצְאֵי יֶרֶךְ-יַעֲקֹב--שִׁבְעִים נָפֶשׁ; וְיוֹסֵף, הָיָה בְמִצְרָיִם.
ו וַיָּמָת יוֹסֵף וְכָל-אֶחָיו, וְכֹל הַדּוֹר הַהוּא.

As you can see, if you count 50 letters, left to right from the last letter of the second word, you get the same thing. TORAH spelled in Hebrew.

One may say that this too is a coincidence. Here is yet a 3rd example of the word Torah spelled within the first few passage of one of the books of the Torah.

Numbers 1: 1-3

א וַיְדַבֵּר יְהוָה אֶל-מֹשֶׁה בְּמִדְבַּר סִינַי, בְּאֹהֶל מוֹעֵד: בְּאֶחָד לַחֹדֶשׁ הַשֵּׁנִי בַּשָּׁנָה הַשֵּׁנִית, לְצֵאתָם מֵאֶרֶץ מִצְרַיִם--לֵאמֹר.

ב שְׂאוּ, אֶת-רֹאשׁ כָּל-עֲדַת בְּנֵי-יִשְׂרָאֵל, לְמִשְׁפְּחֹתָם, לְבֵית אֲבֹתָם--בְּמִסְפַּר שֵׁמוֹת, כָּל-זָכָר לְגֻלְגְּלֹתָם.

ג מִבֶּן עֶשְׂרִים שָׁנָה וָמַעְלָה, כָּל-יֹצֵא צָבָא בְּיִשְׂרָאֵל--תִּפְקְדוּ אֹתָם לְצִבְאֹתָם, אַתָּה וְאַהֲרֹן.

If you count 50 letters from the last letter of the 4th letter you will find the word Torah spelled backwards. So, as you can see, this is no longer within the realms of coincidence. In 3 cases and in 3 books of the Torah, the word Torah is spelled out in code within the first few verses. And yes, it does apply to Deuteronomy as well. But for the sake of brevity we will proceed.

So why the number 50? This is no coincidence, 50 is important in Judaism. Every 50th year is a jubilee year; and the Torah itself was revealed to Moses 50 days after the Exodus from Egypt.

If you want to learn more about these Torah codes, please refer to a great book called : The Torah Codes

I could go on and on about this but I wanted to at least show that there is precedence for secrets within the words of the bible, not just Genesis. Another reason I mentioned this is because within the first few verses of Genesis contain the hidden names of God. In the next chapter we will discover them.

CHAPTER 3: THE 6 NAMES OF CREATION

We will now discuss the 6 names of creation. They are hidden with the first few verses of Genesis. Who discovered these names is unknown, but this secret has passed along from generation to generation amongst a very small group of people who are steeped within this great and most perfect science of the occult mysteries. At first this was passed down through devote Jewish Kabbalists, but then spread out to mystic Christians as well around the high middle ages. As I said, you will not find any mention of this online. I learned of this by mere chance. I have a friend who is one of the most famous writers on Kabbalah in modern times. He , himself, is not a mystic but he has access to all things Kabbalah. I was astonished to see some of the original works that he has. For the sake of this text I cant mention his name, but if you look closely at the books that are available on Kabbalah these days, you will most certainly see his name. When I saw the information about the 6 names of God in genesis I asked him why he didn't write a book on it. He was not interested and wanted to focus more on the history of Kabbalah and not practical application. Fair enough. So now, I will write it here.

As we discussed in the previous chapter, the Torah codes are astounding. Although I covered just 3 , there are countless others that are simply mind boggling. The bible is truly a secret code book, as are every other spiritual text. As I mentioned in my first book "The 72 Names Of God", . There are several levels of biblical study. One of which is the Secret level. Torah codes and what you are about to learn is of that level.

The 6 name of Creation can be cleaned from the first Paragraph of Genesis. Here is the Hebrew and then English translation.

Genesis 1: 1-4

א בְּרֵאשִׁית, בָּרָא אֱלֹהִים, אֵת הַשָּׁמַיִם, וְאֵת הָאָרֶץ.

ב וְהָאָרֶץ, הָיְתָה תֹהוּ וָבֹהוּ, וְחֹשֶׁךְ, עַל-פְּנֵי תְהוֹם; וְרוּחַ אֱלֹהִים, מְרַחֶפֶת עַל-פְּנֵי הַמָּיִם.

ג וַיֹּאמֶר אֱלֹהִים, יְהִי אוֹר; וַיְהִי-אוֹר.

ד וַיַּרְא אֱלֹהִים אֶת-הָאוֹר, כִּי-טוֹב; וַיַּבְדֵּל אֱלֹהִים, בֵּין הָאוֹר וּבֵין הַחֹשֶׁךְ.

English:

1 In the beginning God created the heavens and the earth. [2] Now the earth was formless and empty, darkness was over the surface of the deep, and the Spirit of God was hovering over the waters.

[3] And God said, "Let there be light," and there was light. [4] God saw that the light was good, and he separated the light from the darkness.

The first 4 verses are significant because it describes that primordial light and darkness we discussed earlier. All of creation comes froth from this Yin and Yang of light and darkness and these the 6 names are gleaned from those same verses.

As with the Torah Codes, we will be gleaning the names using 50 letter equidistant letters. The root word that we will begin with is the first word of the book. Each name of the 6 names starts with that first word.

Name 1

א בְּרֵאשִׁית, בָּרָא אֱלֹהִים, אֵת הַשָּׁמַיִם, וְאֵת הָאָרֶץ.

ב וְהָאָרֶץ, הָיְתָה תֹהוּ וָבֹהוּ, וְחֹשֶׁךְ, עַל-פְּנֵי תְהוֹם; וְרוּחַ אֱלֹהִים, מְרַחֶפֶת עַל-פְּנֵי הַמָּיִם.

ג וַיֹּאמֶר אֱלֹהִים, יְהִי אוֹר; וַיְהִי-אוֹר.

ד וַיַּרְא אֱלֹהִים אֶת-הָאוֹר, כִּי-טוֹב; וַיַּבְדֵּל אֱלֹהִים, בֵּין הָאוֹר וּבֵין הַחֹשֶׁךְ.

א פ ב

PRONOUNCED BA-PA

Name 2

א בְּרֵאשִׁית, בָּרָא אֱלֹהִים, אֵת הַשָּׁמַיִם, וְאֵת הָאָרֶץ.

ב וְהָאָרֶץ, הָיְתָה תֹהוּ וָבֹהוּ, וְחֹשֶׁךְ, עַל-פְּנֵי תְהוֹם; וְרוּחַ אֱלֹהִים, מְרַחֶפֶת עַל-פְּנֵי הַמָּיִם.

ג וַיֹּאמֶר אֱלֹהִים, יְהִי אוֹר; וַיְהִי-אוֹר.

ד וַיַּרְא אֱלֹהִים אֶת-הָאוֹר, כִּי-טוֹב; וַיַּבְדֵּל אֱלֹהִים, בֵּין הָאוֹר וּבֵין הַחֹשֶׁךְ.

רנר

PRONOUNCED RA-NAR

Name 3

א בְּרֵאשִׁית, בָּרָא אֱלֹהִים, אֵת הַשָּׁמַיִם, וְאֵת הָאָרֶץ.

ב וְהָאָרֶץ, הָיְתָה תֹהוּ וָבֹהוּ, וְחֹשֶׁךְ, עַל-פְּנֵי תְהוֹם; וְרוּחַ אֱלֹהִים, מְרַחֶפֶת עַל-פְּנֵי הַמָּיִם.

ג וַיֹּאמֶר אֱלֹהִים, יְהִי אוֹר; וַיְהִי-אוֹר.

ד וַיַּרְא אֱלֹהִים אֶת-הָאוֹר, כִּי-טוֹב; וַיַּבְדֵּל אֱלֹהִים, בֵּין הָאוֹר וּבֵין הַחֹשֶׁךְ.

א י ו

PRONOUNCED EYE-VA

Name 4

א בְּרֵאשִׁית, בָּרָא אֱלֹהִים, אֵת הַשָּׁמַיִם, וְאֵת הָאָרֶץ.

ב וְהָאָרֶץ, הָיְתָה תֹהוּ וָבֹהוּ, וְחֹשֶׁךְ, עַל-פְּנֵי תְהוֹם; וְרוּחַ אֱלֹהִים, מְרַחֶפֶת עַל-פְּנֵי הַמָּיִם.

ג וַיֹּאמֶר אֱלֹהִים, יְהִי אוֹר; וַיְהִי-אוֹר.

ד וַיַּרְא אֱלֹהִים אֶת-הָאוֹר, כִּי-טוֹב; וַיַּבְדֵּל אֱלֹהִים, בֵּין הָאוֹר וּבֵין הַחֹשֶׁךְ.

שׁתי

PRONOUNCED SHAT-EYE

Name 5

א בְּרֵאשִׁית, בָּרָא אֱלֹהִים, אֵת הַשָּׁמַיִם, וְאֵת הָאָרֶץ.

ב וְהָאָרֶץ, הָיְתָה תֹהוּ וָבֹהוּ, וְחֹשֶׁךְ, עַל-פְּנֵי תְהוֹם; וְרוּחַ אֱלֹהִים, מְרַחֶפֶת עַל-פְּנֵי הַמָּיִם.

ג וַיֹּאמֶר אֱלֹהִים, יְהִי אוֹר; וַיְהִי-אוֹר.

ד וַיַּרְא אֱלֹהִים אֶת-הָאוֹר, כִּי-טוֹב; וַיַּבְדֵּל אֱלֹהִים, בֵּין הָאוֹר וּבֵין הַחֹשֶׁךְ.

י ה ר

PRONOUNCED YAH-RE

Name 6

א בְּרֵאשִׁית, בָּרָא אֱלֹהִים, אֵת הַשָּׁמַיִם, וְאֵת הָאָרֶץ.

ב וְהָאָרֶץ, הָיְתָה תֹהוּ וָבֹהוּ, וְחֹשֶׁךְ, עַל-פְּנֵי תְהוֹם; וְרוּחַ אֱלֹהִים, מְרַחֶפֶת עַל-פְּנֵי הַמָּיִם.

ג וַיֹּאמֶר אֱלֹהִים, יְהִי אוֹר; וַיְהִי-אוֹר.

ד וַיַּרְא אֱלֹהִים אֶת-הָאוֹר, כִּי-טוֹב; וַיַּבְדֵּל אֱלֹהִים, בֵּין הָאוֹר וּבֵין הַחֹשֶׁךְ.

א ו ת

PRONOUNCED TOW-AH

THE NAMES AGAIN

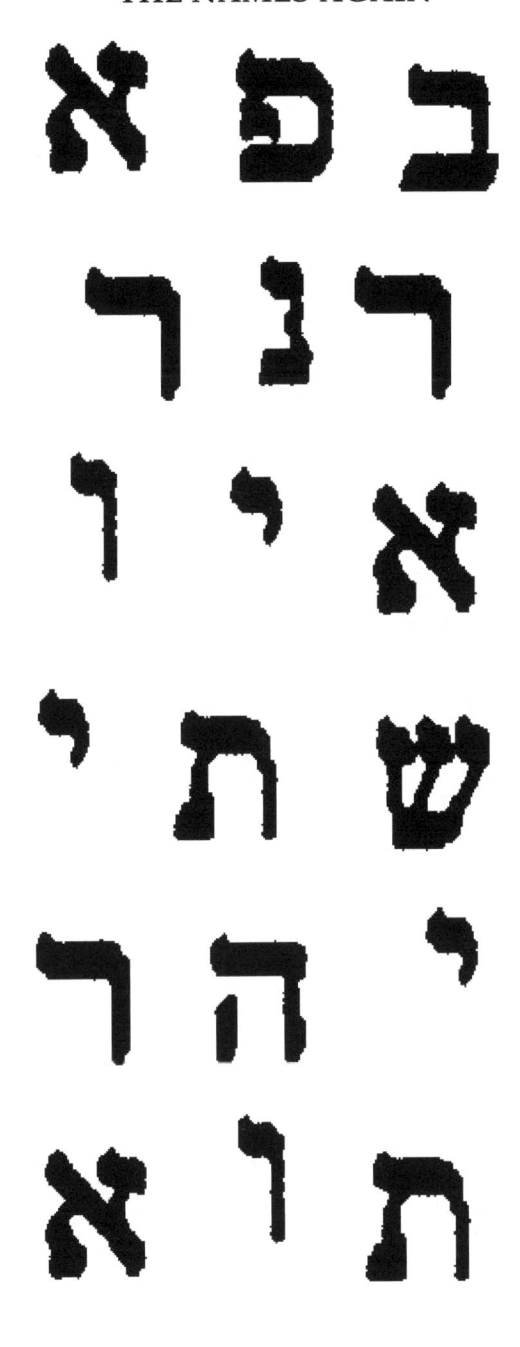

א	פ	בְּ
ר	נ	ר
ו	י	אָ
י	ת	שׁ
ר	ה	יְ
א	ו	ת

As you can see, the name start with each successive letter of the first word of Genesis. The first word in Hebrew is pronounced Be-Re-Sheet. Which means, as you know " In the beginning" . At first I was wondering why the names started with each letter and then it dawned on me. The word "in the beginning" is a powerful word. It's the first word of manifestation. A word of powerful new beginnings and fresh starts.

In the next chapter, I will take you through 6 exercise, 1 for each name.

CHAPTER 4: THE POWER OF THE 6

In this chapter we will go through 6 exercises, 1 for each name. Each name represents a different aspect of life. Mainly and in order:

Spiritual
Physical
Mental
Emotional
Social
Financial

Exercise 1 - Spiritual

א בְּרֵאשִׁית, בָּרָא אֱלֹהִים, אֵת הַשָּׁמַיִם, וְאֵת הָאָרֶץ.

ב וְהָאָרֶץ, הָיְתָה תֹהוּ וָבֹהוּ, וְחֹשֶׁךְ, עַל-פְּנֵי תְהוֹם; וְרוּחַ אֱלֹהִים, מְרַחֶפֶת עַל-פְּנֵי הַמָּיִם.

ג וַיֹּאמֶר אֱלֹהִים, יְהִי אוֹר; וַיְהִי-אוֹר.

ד וַיַּרְא אֱלֹהִים אֶת-הָאוֹר, כִּי-טוֹב; וַיַּבְדֵּל אֱלֹהִים, בֵּין הָאוֹר וּבֵין הַחֹשֶׁךְ.

א פ ב

PRONOUNCED BA-PA

STEP 1: Let your eyes roam over the Hebrew letters in the above passage of Genesis while thinking of your need to make a spiritual connection to source.

STEP 2: Imagine the letters of the name glowing in your mind's eye

STEP 3: Say the Name BA-PA

STEP 4: Sit in silent as you imagine the letters permeate your being.

You will feel a shift from this.

End of Exercise 1.

Exercise 2 - Physical

א בְּרֵאשִׁית, בָּרָא אֱלֹהִים, אֵת הַשָּׁמַיִם, וְאֵת הָאָרֶץ.

ב וְהָאָרֶץ, הָיְתָה תֹהוּ וָבֹהוּ, וְחֹשֶׁךְ, עַל-פְּנֵי תְהוֹם; וְרוּחַ אֱלֹהִים, מְרַחֶפֶת עַל-פְּנֵי הַמָּיִם.

ג וַיֹּאמֶר אֱלֹהִים, יְהִי אוֹר; וַיְהִי-אוֹר.

ד וַיַּרְא אֱלֹהִים אֶת-הָאוֹר, כִּי-טוֹב; וַיַּבְדֵּל אֱלֹהִים, בֵּין הָאוֹר וּבֵין הַחֹשֶׁךְ.

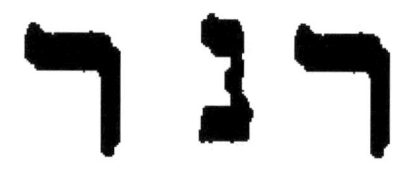

ר נ ר

PRONOUNCED RA-NAR

STEP 1: Let your eyes roam over the Hebrew letters in the above passage of Genesis while thinking of whatever physical issues you may have. Could be a weight loss goal as well. Make it about the body.

STEP 2: Imagine the letters of the name glowing in your mind's eye

STEP 3: Say the Name RA - NAR

STEP 4: Sit in silent as you imagine the letters permeate your being, see the letters infuse your body with healing light.

You will feel a shift from this.

End of Exercise 2.

Exercise 3 - Mental

א בְּרֵאשִׁית, בָּרָא אֱלֹהִים, אֵת הַשָּׁמַיִם, וְאֵת הָאָרֶץ.

ב וְהָאָרֶץ, הָיְתָה תֹהוּ וָבֹהוּ, וְחֹשֶׁךְ, עַל-פְּנֵי תְהוֹם; וְרוּחַ אֱלֹהִים, מְרַחֶפֶת עַל-פְּנֵי הַמָּיִם.

ג וַיֹּאמֶר אֱלֹהִים, יְהִי אוֹר; וַיְהִי-אוֹר.

ד וַיַּרְא אֱלֹהִים אֶת-הָאוֹר, כִּי-טוֹב; וַיַּבְדֵּל אֱלֹהִים, בֵּין הָאוֹר וּבֵין הַחֹשֶׁךְ.

א י ו

PRONOUNCED EYE-VA

STEP 1: Let your eyes roam over the Hebrew letters in the above passage of Genesis while thinking of whatever mental issues or mental stress you may have. This is very good against anxiety and depression

STEP 2: Imagine the letters of the name glowing in your mind's eye

STEP 3: Say the Name EYE-VA

STEP 4: Sit in silent as you imagine the letters permeate your head. Watch how the letters of God heal your mind.

You will feel a shift from this.

End of Exercise 3.

Exercise 4 - Emotional

א בְּרֵאשִׁית, בָּרָא אֱלֹהִים, אֵת הַשָּׁמַיִם, וְאֵת הָאָרֶץ.

ב וְהָאָרֶץ, הָיְתָה תֹהוּ וָבֹהוּ, וְחֹשֶׁךְ, עַל-פְּנֵי תְהוֹם; וְרוּחַ אֱלֹהִים, מְרַחֶפֶת עַל-פְּנֵי הַמָּיִם.

ג וַיֹּאמֶר אֱלֹהִים, יְהִי אוֹר; וַיְהִי-אוֹר.

ד וַיַּרְא אֱלֹהִים אֶת-הָאוֹר, כִּי-טוֹב; וַיַּבְדֵּל אֱלֹהִים, בֵּין הָאוֹר וּבֵין הַחֹשֶׁךְ.

שׁ ת י

PRONOUNCED SHAT-EYE

STEP 1: Let your eyes roam over the Hebrew letters in the above passage of Genesis while thinking of whatever emotional issues you might be having. Very good to keep you emotionally grounded

STEP 2: Imagine the letters of the name glowing and relaxing your body and mind. Let the letters swirl around you.

STEP 3: Say the Name SHAT-EYE

STEP 4: Sit in silent as you imagine the letters permeate your head. Watch how the letters of God heal your emotional state

You will feel a shift from this.

End of Exercise 4.

Exercise 5 - Social

א בְּרֵאשִׁית, בָּרָא אֱלֹהִים, אֵת הַשָּׁמַיִם, וְאֵת הָאָרֶץ.

ב וְהָאָרֶץ, הָיְתָה תֹהוּ וָבֹהוּ, וְחֹשֶׁךְ, עַל-פְּנֵי תְהוֹם; וְרוּחַ אֱלֹהִים, מְרַחֶפֶת עַל-פְּנֵי הַמָּיִם.

ג וַיֹּאמֶר אֱלֹהִים, יְהִי אוֹר; וַיְהִי-אוֹר.

ד וַיַּרְא אֱלֹהִים אֶת-הָאוֹר, כִּי-טוֹב; וַיַּבְדֵּל אֱלֹהִים, בֵּין הָאוֹר וּבֵין הַחֹשֶׁךְ.

י ה ר

PRONOUNCED YAH-RE

STEP 1: Let your eyes roam over the Hebrew letters in the above passage of Genesis while thinking of whatever social issues you may have. This name is very good for shy people.

STEP 2: Imagine the letters of the name glowing and relaxing your body and mind. Imagine a social situations you are going to be in and imagine the letters instilling courage in you

STEP 3: Say the Name YAH-RE

STEP 4: Sit in silent as you imagine the letters permeate your head. Watch how the letters of God heal your social issue

You will feel a shift from this.

End of Exercise 5.

Exercise 6 - Financial

א בְּרֵאשִׁית, בָּרָא אֱלֹהִים, אֵת הַשָּׁמַיִם, וְאֵת הָאָרֶץ.
ב וְהָאָרֶץ, הָיְתָה תֹהוּ וָבֹהוּ, וְחֹשֶׁךְ, עַל-פְּנֵי תְהוֹם; וְרוּחַ אֱלֹהִים, מְרַחֶפֶת עַל-פְּנֵי הַמָּיִם.
ג וַיֹּאמֶר אֱלֹהִים, יְהִי אוֹר; וַיְהִי-אוֹר.
ד וַיַּרְא אֱלֹהִים אֶת-הָאוֹר, כִּי-טוֹב; וַיַּבְדֵּל אֱלֹהִים, בֵּין הָאוֹר וּבֵין הַחֹשֶׁךְ.

ת ו א

PRONOUNCED TOW-AH

STEP 1: Let your eyes roam over the Hebrew letters in the above passage of Genesis while thinking of your financial request.

STEP 2: Imagine the letters of the name glowing all around you. Feel the letters making you abundant.

STEP 3: Say the Name TOW-AH

STEP 4: Sit in silent as you imagine the letters permeate your body. Imagine being prosperous financially.

You will feel a shift from this.

End of Exercise 6.

That is the end of the exercises. As you can see, these are very simple exercises, they do not need to be hard. In fact manifestation is not about making things hard, but easier. The names you have just learned can be used for all areas of your life and in any way you desire. Yes, like all energy, these names can be used for dark purposes as well. They are, after all , names of creation.

CONCLUSION

It may not seem like it, but what you have just learned has been secret for many years. It has now come to light. Many people expect that this knowledge to be overly complex, but it isn't. I believe one of the reasons it has not come to light sooner is because it isn't fancy and complicated like other kabbalistic practices.   Please note, you can use these names to CREATE ANYTHING you want. What you have experienced in the exercises chapter is but a very very small sample of what can be done. These are literally the names of creation. CREATE whatever it is you want. The names are manifestation engines

But remember...

Be careful what you ask for, you just might get it.

Printed in Great
Britain
by Amazon